SAINT FOR THE AFFLICTED

Saint Dymphna

Patron Saint of Nervous and Mental Patients

BY LAWRENCE G. LOVASIK, S.V.D.

DIVINE WORD MISSIONARY PUBLICATIONS
Techny, Illinois

FOREWORD

The most serious medical problem facing our nation is that presented by nervous and mental diseases. About eight million persons are thus afflicted. One out of every twenty persons in the United States is emotionally or mentally maladjusted and needs treatment for some personality disorder. More than half the patients who visit their family doctor for some physical ailment are really suffering from some type of emotional disorder. *Nervous and mental disease takes a larger toll than do cancer, infantile paralysis, and tuberculosis combined.* More than half of all the hospital beds in this country are occupied by mental patients.

These are startling facts and present the reason for the need of this booklet. We need a patron for people suffering from nervous and mental diseases. There is such a patron but not many people in the United States have even heard of her. She is Saint Dymphna. These pages will tell her story.

May devotion to Saint Dymphna (pronounced: dímf-na) become a source of hope not only for those suffering from mental and nervous illness, but also for those whose friends and loved ones are so afflicted. May Our Lady, Health of the Sick and Comforter of the Afflicted, bring this message where it is needed most.

FATHER LAWRENCE G. LOVASIK, S.V.D.
Sacred Heart Mission Seminary
Girard, Pennsylvania

I. SAINT FOR THE AFFLICTED

Virgin and Martyr

Catholics for the most part are entirely unfamiliar with many of the glorious saints of Ireland. One such forgotten or unknown saint, who, on account of her spotless virtue and glorious martyrdom, is sometimes referred to as the "Lily of Eire," is St. Dymphna.

Many details of the life of St. Dymphna are lacking, but the outstanding facts of her short life, as well as the many miracles worked through her intercession after her death, are well known. Her life was written by a certain Peter, a Canon Regular of St. Autbert's Church in Cambray, France, in 1680. Other writers before him have written about her and entertained almost tender devotion toward her.

Dymphna was born in the seventh century, when Ireland was almost universally Catholic. Yet, strange to say, her father, Damon, a petty king or chieftain of Oriel, was a pagan. He was a man of great wealth and power, acquired by his success in many wars. Her mother was also of noble descent, exceptionally beautiful, and a devout Christian. Dymphna herself is said to have borne a striking resemblance to her mother and to have inherited both her beauty and charm of disposition. She was a most sweet and winsome child. Every affection and attention was lavished on her from birth. Heaven, too, favored her with special graces.

Dymphna was fourteen when tragedy struck the household. Her mother died and her father is said to have been afflicted with a mental illness, brought on by his grief. The girl was entrusted to the care of a devout Christian woman, who prepared her for Baptism. Father Gerebran, an old and venerable priest, baptized her. He was evidently a member of the household and later taught Dymphna her letters along with the truths of religion. A bright and eager pupil, she advanced rapidly in wisdom and grace. When still very young, Dymphna, like so many other noble Irish maidens before and after her, being filled with a deep love for Jesus Christ, chose Him for her Divine Spouse and consecrated her virginity to Him and to His Blessed Mother by a vow of chastity.

In a frantic effort to fill the void in his life caused by the death of his wife, Dymphna's father sent messengers throughout his own and other lands to find some woman of noble birth, resembling his beloved wife, who would be willing to marry him. Their search was fruitless. Very likely filled with fear of punishments, they proposed another plan. They directed the king's attention to the remarkable resemblance between Dymphna and her mother, both in physical beauty and charm of disposition, and suggested that he propose marriage to her.

Under the stress of mental illness and passion, the king was willing to follow this scandalous proposal. He tried to persuade Dymphna by promises of riches and flattering words. But she was filled with disgust by the persistent advances of her father, not only because she saw the evil of such a marriage, but also because she had already dedicated herself to a life of virginity and would have rejected marriage under any circumstances.

Dymphna laid the matter before Father Gerebran and upon his advice decided to flee from her homeland. He himself agreed to accompany her, together with two other friends, the court jester and his wife. The little group hurried to the coast. Faithful vassals rowed them across the mist-laden North Sea. They landed upon the Belgian coast near Antwerp. Fleeing inland, the fugitives made their way to Gelium — now Gheel — where hospitable villagers received the Celtic strangers into their homes. They found here a chapel dedicated to St. Martin of Tours, and decided to make their home near it. Dymphna soon made herself beloved by her tender care of the sick and poor.

Damon, very angry at the disappearance of his daughter, immediately set out in search of the fugitives. They were eventually traced to Belgium. When Dymphna's father tried to persuade her to return with him, Father Gerebran rebuked him for his wicked proposal. In order to break down her resistance, the king gave orders that Father Gerebran should be put to death. Without delay, his wicked retainers laid violent hands upon the priest. With one blow of a sword his head was severed from his shoulders.

The death of her beloved spiritual guide only confirmed Dymphna's resolution to resist unto blood if needs be, herself. Her father again tried to persuade her to return to Ireland with him. This time she not only refused but even scorned his cruel threats. Infuriated by her resistance, he drew his sword and struck off the head of his daughter. She was then only fifteen years of age. Dymphna received the crown of martyrdom between the years 620 and 640.

The records of Dymphna's life and death say that the bodies of the two martyrs lay on the ground for quite some time before the inhabitants of Gheel removed them to a cave. Some years later a more suitable burial place was sought. When the workingmen, assigned to the task, entered the cave and cleared away the rubble, they discovered two beautifully sculptured tombs of pure white stone. They opened Dymphna's coffin and found lying over her breast a red tile bearing the inscription: "Here lies the body of the holy virgin and martyr, Dymphna." Her remains were placed in a small church of the town and kept there for many years.

Patroness of Nervous and Mental Patients

Dymphna died to save her virginity from a violently insane father. Her martyrdom bears a striking resemblance to that of St. Maria Goretti in our own century. So deep was the love of Dymphna for her unfor-

6

tunate parent that she has spent her time in heaven curing mentally ill people. She has for this reason rightly deserved the title of the patron saint of those suffering from nervous ailments and mental afflictions.

.The devout Catholic villagers of Gheel diagnosed the unnatural father as insane while they labelled Dymphna "Saint" and erected a shrine over her remains. The relics of her body were placed in a golden reliquary and transferred to the magnificent church of St. Dymphna, which was built upon the site of the original burial place. Many miracles began to occur at her shrine. On one occasion a violently insane person was brought to the church and blessed with Dymphna's relics and was instantly cured. Novenas and applications of her relics brought about many other reported cures. These devotions and wonders continue to this day. Then began those strange pilgrimages of the deranged to pray at Dymphna's shrine. When they brought their delusions and obsessions to be laid at the tomb of the martyred virgin, they were tenderly cared for by the hospitable villagers. Many of the pilgrims recovered their mental health, as is attested by the ancient records of the community which are still preserved.

This good work had been going on for many years when William, Bishop of Cambray, in 1247, caused an investigation of these remarkable cures. This resulted in the founding of the Infirmary of St. Elizabeth at Gheel, an institution in charge of the nuns of St. Augustine, who were brought from Mechlin, a city in north central Belgium. The Infirmary served as a place to care for mentally afflicted persons during their stay in Gheel.

Pilgrimages continued throughout the Middle Ages. Gradually it became an established custom for the pilgrims to remain in village homes while awaiting recovery. The villagers, who seemed to have a sixth sense in handling their strange guests, accepted their vocation as a religious duty.

Canon Peter states in his history of St. Dymphna's life: "We can hardly question the efficacy of her intercession being manifested by signs and wonders, frequently wrought among the people who had selected her as their special patroness."

In 1316 Pope John XXII, in 1410 Pope John XXIII, and in 1431 Pope Eugenius IV testified in Apostolic Documents to the miracles worked through the intercession of Dymphna. She was canonized a saint and May 15 was set as her feast in commemoration of the day on which she was martyred. Her feastday is a national holiday in Belgium and is celebrated with great festivity.

Thus Sovereign Pontiffs and the Bishops have always shown their veneration for St. Dymphna and have favored with indulgences the church which is built over the saint's tomb — the tomb which God has favored with so many miracles wrought through her intercession. The afflicted and their friends who have invoked the name of St. Dymphna have not found her wanting. Since she resisted courageously the insane, raging love of her father, God has made her the special protectress of all who are afflicted with nervous and mental disorders, and many miraculous cures at Gheel have established her in that title.

In 1636 Pope Urban VIII blessed and indulgenced the reestablished Confraternity of St. Dymphna, which exists today. Knowing of what had been done by the Confraternity of St. Dymphna through the centuries, the late Archbishop John T. McNicholas, of Cincinnati, Ohio, considered it an ideal Confraternity to take over the apostolate of the nervous and insane in our own country. On June 23, 1940, a chapel to St. Dymphna was dedicated on the Longview Hospital grounds, Cincinnati, and a League in her honor which offers many spiritual benefits has been established by the Archbishop. Dues paid by the members of the League of St. Dymphna are used by the director to provide Catholic books and reading material for the patients, and to provide reading glasses, hearing aids and dentures, which are not provided by the state. Some of the funds have also been used to decorate the chapel of St. Dymphna on the hospital grounds. The Confraternity has not done what the Archbishop had hoped for it, but the 1,500 members who have joined have illustrated what can be accomplished when lay apostles set their minds to help the most unfortunate people among us — the mentally ill. Further information about the League of St. Dymphna, as well as pictures and medals, may be obtained from: *St. Dymphna Chapel, Longview Hospital, Cincinnati 16, Ohio.*

In state hospitals for mentally ill throughout the United States and Canada many perpetual Novenas (all well attended) are going on. Very interesting cases can be reported, in which the prayers have been answered and restoration to normal health achieved. All this is a manifestation of the miraculous mercy of God through the intercession of St. Dymphna. Devotion to this saint is spreading very rapidly. We of this day especially have great need of the intercession of St. Dymphna.

The Gheel Plan

The spot on which St. Dymphna died at Gheel, Belgium, now houses one of the greatest (if not the greatest) medical centers in the world for care and treatment of mentally sick people. Since the thirteenth century it has been their haven of refuge. The population of the town today is only about 18,000, of which about 3,000 are patients. A goodly number of these, if not an actual majority, are being cared for in the homes of the townspeople themselves.

The pilgrimages to the Shrine of St. Dymphna began in the seventh century and continued throughout the Middle Ages. For generations it has come to be recognized as a sign of good standing in the community to have, or have had patients in one's home. Nearly all the inhabitants of the town of Gheel are members of St. Dymphna's League and as such do all they can to assist in the cure of the patients. Religious orders established guest houses at Gheel for the deranged pilgrims; the city councilors erected comfortable brick cottages for the disturbed and the indigent. Thus began that intelligent and benevolent interest in the care of the mentally sick which continues to this day and has culminated in the famous Belgian Family Care Colonies, the great contribution made by Catholicism to psychiatry, which is now being practiced in all major European countries and in North and South America. Belgium has 4 State Colonies, with 5,000 patients.

For centuries the treatment of the mentally afflicted has been directed almost entirely by the Church, because of the traditional origin and early development of the Colony on a religious basis. Since 1852, with the large increase in the number of patients, the Colonies have been operated by the Belgian government, with a full corps of psychiatrists and registered nurses to supervise the carefully selected foster-families and their "guests." But the hardest job has fallen to the religious orders. They operate 47 small closed hospitals, with from 50 to 800 beds each. These accept only the acutely ill and deteriorated, who comprise 80% of the total mentally ill population. But even here the Catholic spirit is visible.

Instead of the bare, stiff, official atmosphere and impersonalized care of the American state hospital, Belgian religious organize and furnish their hospitals to resemble the Flemish middle-class home. The home atmosphere, replete with pictures and flowers, provides continuity for the life-experiences of the patient and minimizes the accent on illness.

As the acutely ill improve, they are transferred to one of the State Colonies to be placed with foster-families and gradually oriented to normal social and economic life. The Catholic element of charity is in the marked cordiality existing between social worker, patients, and foster-parents. Religious orders also maintain "open hospitals," or psychopathic institutes, where persons who realize they are mentally slipping may voluntarily apply for psychiatric treatment without the emotional scare of legal commitment. There is also a network of mental hygiene clinics which cover the country, where the mildly affected may obtain treatments without leaving their homes. Five welfare agencies co-operate with the government in setting up rehabilitation centers, where recovered patients may get help in making a stable comeback.

We are obliged to admit the spiritual element in these recoveries for which Gheel is famous: faith and hope are aroused within demented minds: and charity, which inspires the hospitality of the devout people of Gheel, makes them discern the dignity of the human person behind the distorted mask of madness. And all this began in an era when, elsewhere in Europe, the insane were driven out to beg, chained in cages, or exhibited at fairs, as curiosities.

And today, while the great nations, our own in particular, stand red-faced and self-accused before the bar of public opinion, and admit their neglect of the mentally ill, little Belgium has gone quietly on her way perfecting her Catholic — and common-sense — system for the prevention and treatment of mental ills. So efficacious is the Catholic method that, among progressive countries with modern hospital facilities, Belgium's rate for mental hospital population is the lowest in the world. In the treatment of mentally ill the Catholics in Belgium have been over 1,000 years ahead of the times, and the so-called "modern psychiatry" is just now catching on and up.

There is a vast difference between the "ideal" sanatoriums at Gheel, where the newest and most advanced medical methods of treatment are combined with a deep sense of religion, and our own mental institutions in this country. Gheel stands as a challenge to our American institutions for the mentally ill. We spend millions, but Gheel gets results. This could mean that it is religion rather than money that we lack.

Our foremost medical authorities commend the Gheel plan. Its soundness and principles are today more widely recognized than ever before. Many ranking psychiatrists

13

visit Gheel annually to study the methods used at St. Elizabeth Sanatorium. Writing in the *American Journal of Psychiatry* in 1936, *Dr. Kilgore* gave a glowing account of all he witnessed at Gheel, but added, "It may be impossible elsewhere to develop a system exactly as it is conducted at Gheel. The religious element which played such a big part in its early history cannot be made to order. St. Dymphnas are uncommon today."

The relation between religion and a stable mentality was expressed by *Dr. Frederic Sano,* internationally known psychiatrist, formerly director of the State Colony at Gheel, in these words: "The Belgian hospital and family care system were originally founded upon Catholic religious principles, and while I am a non-believer, yet, as a scientist, I recognize that the faith, hope and charity of religion have important therapeutic values. Moreover, religion has a social value: it salvages the derelicts of society."

The Gheel Colony's social service worker, *Mme. Borgers-Sargent,* graduate of the Antwerp School of Social Service, recently made this statement: "Our 3,000 patients live practically unrestricted lives among the 18,000 population of Gheel. They share freely in the recreation and family life of their foster-parents. The greater number are regularly employed at prevailing wages. Doctors, nurses, and social workers strive to maintain a friendly relationship with each patient which will impress upon his mind, however temporarily unbalanced, a picture of himself as a responsible, normally functioning member of the community. This minimizes his concept of himself as a sick person, and affords him a sense of security. The Catholic treatment of mental disease, barring physical causes, lies in the Catholic thesis of the balanced life, in which the elements of the good life, work, recreation and love of God and of man, have a chance to exert their healing influence."

Mental disease is America's major disaster. It is more serious and widespread than heart disease, cancer, and polio combined. During 1950, one million six hundred thousand Americans spent some time in a mental hospital. An equal number of the mentally or emotionally unbalanced, remain at large and create uncounted domestic and social tragedies. The remedy? Adoption by each state of the major features of the Catholic Belgian pattern — features recommended by the American Psychiatric Association at their May meeting, 1946. There is here an open field for Catholic religious orders and ecclesiastical authority to help solve America's major problem along the lines of Catholic philosophy and psychiatry.

That which the Church has done at Gheel began with St. Dymphna in the dim opening years of the Middle Ages. Gheel provides another example of how the Church has stood foremost in the care of the afflicted and has always taught the necessity of religion and charity, in particular, in advancing and completing the researches of science.

VARIOUS PRAYERS

Prayer for a Cure

Dearest St. Dymphna, great wonder-worker in every affliction of mind and body, I humbly implore your powerful intercession with Jesus through Mary, the Health of the Sick.

You are filled with love and compassion for the thousands of patients brought to your shrine, and for those who cannot come to your shrine but invoke you in their own homes and in hospitals. Show the same love and compassion towards me, your faithful client. The many miracles and cures which have been wrought through your intercession give me great confidence that you will help me in my present illness *(Mention it)*.

Good Saint Dymphna, the fervent faith and devotion of your many clients who are afflicted with the same illness as I am, inspires me to entrust myself to your special care. I trust in you as a child. I am absolutely confident of obtaining my urgent request, if it is for the greater glory of God and the good of my soul. As a proof of my deep gratitude, I promise to love God more, to receive Holy Communion often, and to pray faithfully, especially my rosary. For the sake of Jesus and Mary, whom you loved so earnestly, grant my prayer.

St. Dymphna, young and beautiful, innocent and pure, help me to imitate your love of purity. You chose to be martyred by your own father's sword rather than consent to a single sin of impurity. Give me the same strength and courage in fighting off the temptations of the world, the flesh, and the devil. As you have given all the love of your heart to Jesus, your Divine Spouse, and consecrated your virginity to Him, help me to love God with my whole heart and serve Him faithfully. As you bore the persecution of your father and the sufferings of an exile so patiently, obtain for me the patience I need to accept the cross of my illness and every other trial with loving resignation to the will of God.

St. Dymphna, through your glorious martyrdom for the love of Christ, help me to be loyal to my faith and my God as long as I live. And when the hour of my own death comes, stand at my side and pray for me that I may at last merit the eternal crown of glory in God's Kingdom.

Good Saint Dymphna, I beg you to recommend my request to Mary, the Health of the Sick and Comforter of the Afflicted, that both Mary and you may present it to Jesus, the Divine Physician.

Saint Dymphna, patroness of those who suffer with nervous and mental diseases, beloved child of Jesus and Mary, pray to Them for me and obtain my request *(three times)*.

In honor of Saint Dymphna: Our Father . . . Hail Mary . . . Glory be. . . . Saint Dymphna, Virgin and Martyr, pray for us.

Prayer to Jesus, the Divine Physician

Jesus, Divine Physician, You have created nature and all the wondrous functions of the human body. You are the Master of Your creation. You can and do suspend the laws of nature for those who have faith in Your goodness and entreat You in fervent prayer. You promised that my prayers would be heard when You said, "Ask, and it shall be given you; seek, and you shall find; knock, and it shall be opened to you. For everyone who asks, receives; and he who seeks, finds; and to him who knocks, it shall be opened" (Matt. 7, 7). You also said, "All things whatsoever you ask in prayer, believe that you shall receive, and they shall come to you" (Mark 11, 24). Full of confidence in these promises, I beg You to help me in my present affliction (*Here mention your request*).

Jesus, Divine Physician, during Your lifetime You cured sickness and disease and even raised the dead to life, because people asked You to do so in prayer. I firmly believe that You will hear my prayer also, if this should be the Will of God.

Through the intercession of St. Dymphna, who suffered martyrdom to prove her love for You and to protect her virtue of purity, I ask for the grace to understand more and more the infinite love of Your Sacred Heart for me. I firmly believe that You love me with a love that ordains all things for my own good even though this may be difficult for my nature to bear. It is a love that turns to good all that I may at the moment consider evil. I love Your Heart that loves me so much.

Jesus, Divine Physician, I thank You for being my best Friend in my illness and my Companion in suffering; I thank You for loving me with a Heart human like my own — a Heart that can understand my sorrows and problems since It has experienced all that I must bear; a Heart that can sympathize with me and befriend me in my hour of need; a Heart that can love me with the love of the best of friends. Like a real furnace of fire Your heart burns for me with a love that knows no end because It has its source in the depths of the Godhead. It burns all for me, as if there were no others to share its infinite warmth. Not all the affection You pour out upon countless other souls lessens Your love for me. Even when I forget You and begin to complain in my illness, You pray for me. Even when I disappoint You by trying to shake off the cross You have placed upon my shoulders, You sacrifice Yourself for me at Holy Mass. When I have pain, You are ready to console and strengthen me, for Your Sacred Heart ever calls to me, "Come to Me, all you who labor and are burdened, and I will give you rest" (Matt. 11, 29). Dearest Jesus, Divine Physician, behold how I am burdened with this cross of illness. I come to You and beg You to give me rest.

Jesus, Divine Physician, help me to realize

that it is only through the cross that I can attain to glory; that it is only through suffering that I can possess the kingdom of heaven. Before Your own dear Mother was crowned Queen of heaven, she became the Mother of Sorrows. All the saints suffered during their lifetime. St. Dymphna was persecuted and finally beheaded by her own father. I, too, have been blessed with suffering. This is the only way I can follow You, for You said, "If anyone wishes to come after Me, let him deny himself, and take up his cross and follow Me" (Matt. 16, 24).

Jesus, Divine Physician, I unite myself with You as You offer Yourself during the Holy Sacrifice of the Mass and renew Your Sacrifice of Calvary. Give my heart sentiments like Your own, so that through frequent Holy Communion and prayer I may become holy and pleasing to God, a worthy co-victim with You, and so that all the actions, sufferings, tears, and disappointments of my life may be thus consecrated to You as a sacrifice for the glory of God. Everything that You send me, or permit in my life, whether favorable or unfavorable, sweet or bitter — even this illness which I must bear is acceptable to me, for I have resolved to conform myself to the Divine Will in all things. You invite me to do so, for You said, "Take my yoke upon you . . . My yoke is easy and My burden light" (Matt. 11, 29). May God's Will always be my will! Jesus, Divine Physician, cure me! Amen.

Our Father ... Hail Mary ... Glory be ...
Jesus, Divine Physician, have mercy on us.
Mother of Sorrows, pray for us.
St. Dymphna, the mental saint, pray for us.

Prayer to Our Lady, Health of the Sick

My dearest Mother Mary, I confidently
invoke you as the Health of the Sick. You
are the loving Mother especially of those
who are blessed with a cross of sickness.
Through the intercession of your faithful
servant, St. Dymphna, whom the Church has
chosen as the heavenly Patroness of those
afflicted with nervous and mental disease, I
humbly plead for this favor *(Mention your
request).*

Mother of Perpetual Help, I beg you to
present my petition to your Divine Son. If
you will pray for me, I cannot be refused,
for your prayers before God are all-powerful.
With childlike trust I abandon myself to
God's Holy Will concerning my request.

Sweet Mother of Mercy, I love you; I put
all my confidence in you. I offer to God
through your hands every suffering that I
must bear, with all the love of my heart.
Make every pain an act of love for God, an
act of atonement for my sins, and merito-
rious for the salvation of souls, especially
for my own soul. Teach me patience and
resignation to the Holy Will of God, in
imitation of you, dear Mother of Sorrows.

O my Mother, you are my hope! For the
sake of your beloved Jesus, and through the
intercession of St. Dymphna, whom you

loved so tenderly as to lead her to sainthood, I beg you to grant my prayer. Amen.

℣. Pray for us, Our Lady, Health of the Sick,.

℟. That we may be made worthy of the promises of Christ.

Let us pray:

Grant us, Your servants, we beg You, O Lord God, that we may be blessed with health of soul and body, and by the glorious intercession of the Blessed Virgin Mary, Health of the Sick, be freed from the sorrows of this present life and enjoy everlasting bliss. Through Christ our Lord. Amen.

Prayer for Those Afflicted with Mental Illness

Lord Jesus Christ, You have willed that Saint Dymphna should be invoked by thousands of clients as the patroness of nervous and mental disease and have brought about that her interest in these patients should be an inspiration to and an ideal of charity at her great shrine and throughout the world. Grant that, through the prayers. of this youthful martyr of purity, those who suffer of nervous and mental illness everywhere on earth may be helped and consoled. I recommend to You in particular ... *(Here mention those you wish to pray for).*

Be pleased to hear the prayers of St. Dymphna and of Your Blessed Mother, Health of the Sick and Comforter of the

Afflicted, in behalf of those whom I recommend to the love and compassion of Your Sacred Heart. Give them patience to bear with their affliction and resignation to do Your Divine Will. Give them the consolation they need and especially the cure they so much desire, if it be Your Will. May we all serve Your suffering members with a charity which may merit for us the reward of being united forever in Heaven with You, our Divine Head, Who live and reign with the Father in the unity of the Holy Spirit forever. Amen. _____

O God, we beg You through Your Servant, Saint Dymphna, who sealed with her blood the love she had for You, her Eternal Spouse, to grant relief to those in our midst who suffer from mental afflictions and nervous disorders. Through Christ our Lord. Amen.   (100 days indulgence)

Prayer of Shut-Ins

Dear Jesus, I come in my weakness to ask You to help me to bear patiently my exile from people. I know how happy I ought to be to live the hidden life as You lived it and to share with You the privilege of suffering for the sins of the world. But I am so short-sighted and so cowardly that I shrink from the very sufferings which You have given me the honor to share with You. I would like to be up and around again among people; but if You wish me to remain as I am, please give me the grace to accept this exile so that I may turn each

hour of my loneliness into the golden rungs
of a ladder by which I can climb high into
heaven and bring others — many, many
others — along with me. Amen.

NOVENA
IN HONOR OF ST. DYMPHNA
(Approved by Pope Urban VIII in 1635)*

First Day — for Faith

O God, Source of our salvation, in the
midst of a pagan people, You enlightened
St. Dymphna by the light of the true faith,
which she professed under the guidance of
her holy confessor, Gerebran, with such con-
stancy that she suffered martyrdom. Through
the intercession of these two saints, we beg
You to strengthen the faith which You have
given us, so that by wisely subjecting our
souls to Your Supreme Authority, and by
faithfully conforming our lives according to
our faith, we may honor You with our whole
heart and soul until the hour of our death.
Through Jesus Christ our Lord. Amen.
Our Father. Hail Mary. Glory be. (5 times)

Second Day — for Hope

Almighty and infinitely good God, You
have promised eternal salvation to those who
obey Your commandments and make zealous
use of Your graces. Through the intercession
of St. Dymphna, who fled from the danger

---

* If possible, try to receive the sacraments of
Penance and Holy Eucharist at least once during
this novena.

of sin by leaving the palace of her father, and who, eager to gain eternal salvation, fled to Belgium to live in poverty, we beg You to grant that we also, who are striving for eternal happiness, may overcome all obstacles in the way of virtue and may attain eternal salvation. Through Jesus Christ our Lord. Amen.

Our Father. Hail Mary. Glory be. *(5 times)*

Third Day — for Charity

God of love, You are the most perfect Being and Creator of all that is good and beautiful. Through the intercession of St. Dymphna, who in her youth loved You above all creatures and for Your sake loved her neighbor as herself, as the image and likeness of You, as the price of the Blood of Jesus and as co-heir of heaven, be pleased to help us by Your powerful grace, that we may faithfully fulfill the two great commandments of charity not only in word, but also in action and in truth. Through Jesus Christ our Lord. Amen.

Our Father. Hail Mary. Glory be. *(5 times)*

Fourth Day — for Piety

God, Our Creator and Supreme Master, St. Dymphna served You with great zeal even in her childhood, by hearing Your word with delight, by assisting at Holy Mass with fervent reverence, and by receiving Holy Communion from the hand of St. Gerebran with tender devotion. Through her intercession we beg You to grant us the same virtue of piety so that, having honored You during this life as our Creator, we may possess You hereafter as our final reward. Through Jesus Christ our Lord. Amen.

Our Father. Hail Mary. Glory be. *(5 times)*

Fifth Day — for Prudence

O God, Ruler of the universe, You allowed St. Dymphna to discover a helpful means of avoiding the evil intentions of her father. Through the merits of Your holy servant, be pleased to grant that we may become, according to the words of Jesus, simple as doves and wise as serpents, so that through prudent advice and sound judgment we may recognize what we must avoid and what we must do to achieve the great work of our salvation. Through Jesus Christ our Lord. Amen.

Our Father. Hail Mary. Glory be. *(5 times)*

Sixth Day — for Justice

O God, Source of eternal justice, You inspired St. Dymphna to flee from her country and her father in order to render to You that which was Yours. Through her intercession we beg You to make us seek after justice so that we may perform our duties toward You as we ought. Through Jesus Christ our Lord. Amen.

Our Father. Hail Mary. Glory be. *(5 times)*

Seventh Day — for Fortitude

O God, rewarder of those who remain firm in their good resolutions, you gave St.

Dymphna such a love of virtue that she had the courage to suffer privation, persecution, and even martyrdom. Through her prayers we beg You to grant us fortitude that we may courageously and perseveringly overcome ourselves and finally conquer the enemy of our salvation. Through Jesus Christ our Lord. Amen.

Our Father. Hail Mary. Glory be. *(5 times)*

Eighth Day — for Temperance

O God, You made St. Dymphna resplendent in the virtue of temperance so that she mastered sensual inclinations and used temporal goods prudently. With temperance she combined the beautiful virtues of modesty, docility, and humility. Let us not forget that humility is called the foundation of all virtue because it banishes from the soul pride, the obstacle to grace. Through the intercession of St. Dymphna, we beg You to guide and direct us, so that being preserved from evil and all nervous disorders, we may obey till death the commandments and counsels You have given us. Through Jesus Christ our Lord. Amen.

Our Father. Hail Mary. Glory be. *(5 times)*

Ninth Day — for Chastity

O God, Lover of innocent souls, You gave St. Dymphna the virtue of angelic purity which made her reserved in all her actions, modest in her dress, attentive in her conversation, upright in her character, so that she even shed her blood to preserve this precious

virtue. Through the intercession of St.
Dymphna, we beg You to bestow upon us
the virtue of chastity that we may enjoy
peace of conscience in this life and the pure
eternal joys of heaven hereafter. Through
Jesus Christ our Lord. Amen.

Our Father. Hail Mary. Glory be. *(5 times)*

Litany in Honor of St. Dymphna
(For private use only)

Lord, have mercy on us.
Christ, have mercy on us.
Lord, have mercy on us.
Christ, hear us.
Christ, graciously hear us.
God the Father of Heaven, *have mercy on us.*
God the Son, Redeemer of the world, *have mercy on us.*
God the Holy Ghost, *have mercy on us.*
Holy Trinity, one God, *have mercy on us.*
Holy Mary, Virgin and Mother of God, *pray for us.*
Health of the sick, *pray, etc.*
Comforter of the afflicted,
Help of Christians,
St. Dymphna, virgin and martyr,
St. Dymphna, daughter of royal parents,
St. Dymphna, child of great beauty of soul and body,
St. Dymphna, docile to the lessons of your pious mother,
St. Dymphna, obedient to your saintly confessor,
St. Dymphna, who abandoned the court of

your father to escape the danger of impurity,

St. Dymphna, who chose a life of poverty on earth so that you might lay up treasures in Heaven,

St. Dymphna, who sought strength and consolation at Holy Mass, Holy Communion, and prayer,

St. Dymphna, ardent lover of the Divine Bridegroom,

St. Dymphna, devoted to the Mother of God,

St. Dymphna, beheaded by your own father,

St. Dymphna, martyr of holy purity,

St. Dymphna, brilliant example of Christian youth,

St. Dymphna, renowned for many miracles,

St. Dymphna, glory of Ireland and Belgium,

St. Dymphna, full of compassion for those in need,

St. Dymphna, protectress against all nervous and mental disorders,

St. Dymphna, consoler of the afflicted,

St. Dymphna, friend of the helpless,

St. Dymphna, comforter of the despondent,

St. Dymphna, light of those in mental darkness,

St. Dymphna, patroness of those who suffer with nervous and mental diseases,

That we may love the Lord our God with all our hearts and above all things,

That we may hate sin and avoid all occasion of sin,

That we may carefully preserve the virtue of purity according to our state,

That we may receive the sacraments frequently,

That we may obtain the spirit of prayer,

That we may be humble and obedient, resigning ourselves to God's Holy Will,

That we may learn to have confidence in God during our afflictions,

That we may obtain the grace of final perseverance,

In moments of temptation,

In times of sickness, disease, war, and persecution,

In our last illness,

At the hour of death,

Lamb of God, Who takest away the sins of the world, *spare us, O Lord.*

Lamb of God, Who takest away the sins of the world, *graciously hear us, O Lord.*

Lamb of God, Who takest away the sins of the world, *have mercy on us.*

Pray for us, St. Dymphna,

That we may be made worthy of the promises of Christ.

Let us pray:

O God, since You gave St. Dymphna to Your Church as a model of all virtues, especially holy purity, and willed that she should seal her faith with her innocent blood and perform numerous miracles, grant that we who honor her as patroness of those afflicted with nervous and mental illness, may continue to enjoy her powerful intercession and protection and attain eternal life. Through Christ our Lord. Amen.

II. MENTAL ILLNESS

What is Mental Illness?

Your mind and emotions are closely connected with your body. Mind and body interact. Your physical condition can affect your emotions, and your emotions can affect your physical well being. Doctors have found that more than half of the persons who visit their family physician for treatment of a physical ailment suffer from emotional difficulties which partially explain their physical symptoms. For example, stomach ulcers are frequently connected with worry and anxiety. In such a case, helping the patient overcome his worrying is just as important to his recovery as are proper diet and medical attention.

Mental conflicts cause not only unhappiness, but also wear and tear both emotionally and physically. If they remain for a long time, they finally bring a person to the breaking point. Conflicts, when suppressed, cause the most trouble. Everyone's nervous system has considerable capacity to absorb strain. However, this capacity is not limitless. Everyone has a limit beyond which he cannot go. If this capacity is exceeded, his nervous system "kicks back" in spite of will power or self-control. A person in this condition is so deeply troubled that he can no longer carry on a normal life alone or in society. He is mentally ill.

The term "mentally ill" has been used to include all kinds of mental and emotional conditions, which actually differ in causes, symptoms, and treatment. There are three types of mental illness.

1. NEUROSIS — NERVOUS AND ANXIOUS PEOPLE

Neurosis is one of the most common forms of emotional disorder. About one out of ten of us suffers from such disorders because of an underlying conflict. Most of these conflicts go on inside us without our knowing of their existence. We only know the symptoms: frustration, unhappiness, obsessions, strange compulsions, fears that we cannot account for, ailments that have no physical basis.

Neurotic people can work and take care of their personal affairs. They do need treatment, however, for their own well being. Although neurosis interferes with a person's happiness and efficiency, it does not usually require hospitalization. The majority of neuroses can be treated by private psychiatrists, at out-patient clinics, or, where these are not available, by doctors with psychiatric understanding. Delay in getting treatment will only bring more unhappiness, frustration, and worry.

A good physician or psychiatrist can help us look back of these fears, anxieties, and tensions, show us how they are connected with earlier experiences, and help us resolve our emotional conflicts. Freed of tension, we are able to solve our problems and overcome our frustrations.

We are living in an age of strong sense impressions, high tension, conflicts, frustrations, crises. These are for the most part intimately linked with a person's moral nature and spiritual outlook on life. The work of alleviating the ills with which mankind is afflicted must, therefore, be carried on with due consideration for the *whole* man, body *and spirit,* not body alone. The failures of modern psychology and psychiatry doubtless can often be traced and ascribed to an improper evaluation of the spiritual factor. These sciences must be aided by supernatural help.

Sin is probably the greatest cause of worry and fear. Since the time of Christ, the Catholic Church through the Sacrament of Penance has given the world the greatest remedy for such mental and moral disorders. The psychiatrist in this case is a confessor. He will not only free us from worry and anxiety by his power from God to take away our sins, but he will also relieve our mind by his advice in helping us rid ourselves of unnecessary worry in conscience matters. Confession in the Catholic Church is the best psychiatric treatment a guilty conscience can get. For this reason sensible psychiatrists send patients with moral problems to their priests. Regular confession is a most beneficial means of preserving a sound mind in a sound body. The greatest happiness in the world is peace of mind and a good conscience.

2. MOODY PEOPLE — PSYCHOSIS

Sometimes not only are emotions seriously disturbed, but the mind also becomes confused, and the whole personality is profoundly changed. These more serious types of illness which affect the emotional and mental life are called psychoses. Psychosis is medical term for what we sometimes improperly call "insanity."

The number of people who suffer from psychoses is much smaller than those who have neuroses. But because psychotic symptoms are more pronounced and more dramatic than neurotic symptoms, they are generally better known. Yet even the most severe form of psychosis may develop gradually, and it is sometimes easy to pass it by in the early stages.

We are all more or less subject to changes in mood. When these changes become extreme in nature, doctors regard them as symptoms of a serious form of mental illness called *manic-depressive psychosis.* It accounts for 10 per cent of first admissions to mental hospitals.

Some cases of extreme moodiness seem to be brought on by grief or by an emotional crisis. But persons suffering from the manic-depressive illness become depressed because they feel that they are not attaining the goal which they have set for themselves. Most of them are ambitious. They are over anxious to achieve success, and they often set their ideal far above what they can accomplish. When they find themselves falling short of their ideal, they plunge into the depths of despair.

Many of those who commit suicide because of unrequited love or financial failure are persons who are really mentally ill. They could have recovered and lived useful lives if their relatives had recognized their illness and placed them under treatment in time.

3. THE RETREAT FROM REALITY — SCHIZOPHRENIA

Schizophrenia means a "splitting of the personality" and is one of the most common forms of mental illness found in our mental hospitals. It accounts for about 20 per cent of all patients admitted. These patients are physically in the real world, but mentally they are in a dream world of their own. They have lost contact with reality. For example, a patient may be in a dull state with a complete breakdown of the will to act; he just gazes off into space. Another patient insists that she is the wife of a famous movie actor. Still another believes that people are trying to poison him. No amount of reasoning will change these mistaken notions. The patient clings to them desperately because they satisfy an emotional need, and he cannot seem to check his ideas against the facts. This illness is very real. Probably the cause will be found neither completely in the body nor entirely in the mind, but in both together. Even though we do not know all about the causes of schizophrenia, it can frequently be cured.

WHAT YOU SHOULD KNOW ABOUT MENTAL ILLNESS

1. MENTAL ILLNESS IS COMMON

Mental illness, according to the U. S. Public Health Service, is America's No. 1 health problem. It affects more people than polio, heart disease, and cancer combined. Its victims occupy nearly half of all the hospital beds in the country. In 1948 there were 500,000 patients in state hospitals alone.

One out of every 20 persons in the United States will at some time in his life develop a mental disorder sufficiently serious to require hospitalization. Another 1 in 20 will suffer an emotional disturbance that will interfere with his well-being and general adjustment.

Translated into dollars and cents, the cost of mental illness in lost earnings amounts to almost a billion dollars each year. There are about 558 institutions caring for psychiatric cases. Maintaining such public institutions costs us over $200,000,000 each year.

About half of the average doctor's patients come to him with symptoms related to emotional difficulties.

2. MENTAL ILLNESS IS NOT A DISGRACE

The patient's illness is not due to a "taint," nor is it a reflection on his family. He acts the way he does because he is sick. No one holds a delirious pneumonia patient responsible for his actions. Why should a manic-

depressive be blamed for what he does because illness has lodged in his mind instead
of his lungs?

3. MENTAL ILLNESS IS NOT A
SINGLE DISEASE

Mental illness resembles physical illness
in that it is not one disease but many. It
may take the form of:

a) FUNCTIONAL PSYCHOSES — such
as *schizophrenia or manic-depressive psychosis.* Doctors can describe the symptoms in
terms of disturbance of function, but they
don't know what the causes are. The causes
may be in the patient's early emotional experiences, or in his physical makeup, or in
his environment. However, most scientists
agree that it is in the relationship of all
these that the answer will be found. Functional psychoses account for about 30 per
cent of all patients admitted to mental
hospitals.

b) ORGANIC PSYCHOSES — such as
cerebral arteriosclerosis or *senile dementia.*
These are disorders that occur in old age
when the human machinery begins to run
down. Organic psychoses are responsible for
about 45 per cent of the patients in state
mental hospitals.

Doctors know the causes of organic psychoses because a physical or structural in-
jury to the brain or central nervous system
can be observed. In such cases the cause of
the illness can be traced to alcoholism,
syphilis, brain tumor, hardening of the ar-

37

teries of the brain, or severe infections (such as pneumonia) which cause delirium.

Sometimes mental illness develops as a person ages. High blood pressure can result in a cerebral hemorrhage which damages the brain and may cause mental symptoms. Hardening of the arteries may first manifest itself in the brain. If sufficiently severe, it will interfere with the blood supply and thus deprive the brain of nutrition.

Much of the mental illness in older people is associated with changes in the blood vessel system. Physical deterioration often makes them irresponsible, querulous, and depressed.

4. MENTAL ILLNESS IS NOT NECESSARILY INHERITED

Just as one person may be born with a tendency to diabetes without developing this condition, another may inherit a vulnerable mental constitution and, given favorable circumstances, never become mentally ill. Most psychiatrists are of the opinion that the chances that mental illness will develop are greater in a family where there have been other mental disturbances than in a family with no such history. No one knows to what extent this may be due to inherited tendencies and to what extent it is due to the atmosphere in which the person lives.

5. MENTAL ILLNESS DOES NOT ATTACK WITHOUT WARNING

Tragedy, sudden change in fortune, or financial reverses may bring on a breakdown.

These factors are so dramatic that they seem to cause the breakdown. But they do not cause it. The seed from which mental illness grows is planted long before the symptoms are apparent to the untrained observer. No single crisis is ever wholly responsible for an emotional collapse; it is merely the trigger on a gun that is already loaded.

Only a qualified doctor, preferably a psychiatrist, can diagnose mental illness. However, just as chills and fever give warning of physical illness, marked or prolonged deviations from a person's normal behavior indicate serious mental or emotional disturbances. A person who shows any of the following symptoms over a period of time may need psychiatric care:

1. Lives in a separate world and refuses to face his problems.
2. Has a delusion that people are persecuting him.
3. Has such severe "blues" that he is incapacitated.
4. Suffers agonies of indecision in making up his mind.
5. Has moods that swing like a pendulum between great joy and depression.
6. Insists he is ill although a thorough medical examination reveals nothing physically wrong.
7. Cannot sleep without medication.
8. Is excessively irritable and given to temper outbursts.
9. Loses interest in his appearance, his job, his family.

10. Talks feverishly, skipping from one subject to another.
11. Goes on spending sprees far beyond his means.
12. Is incapacitated by unfounded fears.
13. Hears or sees imaginary things.

6. IF SYMPTOMS ARE RECOGNIZED

Early diagnosis and prompt treatment can make the difference between temporary disability and long hospitalization. The farther the illness has advanced, the more difficult the cure.

If you recognize one or more symptoms mentioned under 5 in anyone in your family, do not try to overlook them. The symptoms may turn out to be unimportant, but let a doctor decide. See that the person gets help. He is often tragically unaware of his condition. If you discuss it with him, he may not listen. He may be panicked. Don't expect him to "snap out of it." He probably won't. Such persons cannot be cheered up, jollied out of their moods, or reasoned with.

Your physician may suggest psychiatric advice. A reputable psychiatrist can help the family physician and the patient's relatives make proper provisions for care and treatment. He will know whether institutional care is needed or desirable. The family should assume responsibility for seeking and following professional advice.

The psychiatrist may refer the sick person to a psychiatric clinic: an out-patient service where there is a psychiatrist in regular attendance. Periodic treatments at such a clinic may offer the patient all the emotional support he needs until he is well enough to go on alone. This may necessitate a temporary move to a locality where such treatment is available. On the other hand, the specialist may consider the patient's symptoms serious enough to warrant immediate hospitalization.

It is not easy to find a qualified psychiatrist in all parts of the country. Only about 6,000 doctors in the United States belong to the American Psychiatric Association. There are only 2,500 psychiatrists who are diplomates of the American Board of Psychiatry and Neurology. Self-styled therapists who advertise in the classified section of the telephone directory are to be shunned like the plague.

Do not insist upon a private hospital without investigation. It does not follow that the most expensive care is necessarily the best. The cost of a good private sanatorium or hospital is beyond the means of the average family. Eighty-seven per cent of those hospitalized for mental illness enter state hospitals where the cost is scaled to the family's income. State mental hospitals are 18 per cent overcrowded and sadly understaffed; not one in the country measures up to all the minimum standards set by the American Psychiatric Association. Yet many state hospitals do as good a job as many of the expensive private hospitals. If you have any doubts, investigate before you decide. Your doctor is the person best qualified to help you decide. · 41

7. HOW MENTAL ILLNESS IS TREATED

Some of the treatments that are in wide use today are the following:

PSYCHOTHERAPY. This is the psychiatrists' chief tool. It is not an attempt to "cure the mind" by good advice, as many people believe. It is the procedure by which the patient himself — with the doctor's help — comes to see his problems more realistically. It is the groundwork that must be laid before the patient can resolve the conflicts that have contributed to his illness. Sometimes this is accomplished by discussions which lead the patient to change his attitudes or decide to work toward different goals. In other cases, the doctor must use a more technical form of psychotherapy.

PSYCHOANALYSIS. One of these is psychoanalysis. In a series of daily to weekly sessions, the doctor encourages the patient to explore his life experiences in minute detail. With the doctor's help, he gains insight into the reasons life has him temporarily defeated. Each full psychoanalysis requires at least 250 hours. This form of psychotherapy is practiced chiefly by private psychiatrists.

NARCOSYNTHESIS. Sometimes psychotherapy is carried on with the patient under the influence of pentathol or sodium amytal. They are strong sedatives which release the memory of painful experiences the patient has repressed. Through re-living these experiences, he is able, with the doctor's encouragement and with help during follow-up interviews, to overcome his anxieties.

GROUP PSYCHOTHERAPY. The psychiatrist meets with several patients whose problems are similar. He leads the discussion, at the same time encouraging the group to talk through their conflicts with one another. It often helps a patient immeasurably to realize others also have problems, some far more serious than his own.

OCCUPATIONAL THERAPY. Under the direction of a professional therapist, the patients knit, paint, and weave. They make furniture, play musical instruments, model with clay, and do leatherwork. As they improve, they move to manual arts — photography, mechanics, radio, woodworking. Working with their hands helps them to focus their attention. It gives them practice in coordinating their movements on projects that are scaled to their ability. Pride in their creations can sometimes do more to restore the self-confidence of patients than any other part of the hospital program. For other patients, the benefit of occupational therapy lies in the experience of working together as a group.

HYDROTHERAPY. The name means "water treatment" in Greek.

(1) *Continuous bath.* The patient lies in a hammock suspended in water kept at body temperature. The length of time the patient remains in the tub depends upon his condition. (2) *Wet pack.* Sheets wrung out in cold water are wrapped snugly around the patient. The sheets are swathed in blankets. They soon adjust to body tempera-

ture, and the patient, thus relaxed, usually sleeps. Both these treatments are designed to soothe the disturbed and the excited. (3) *Needle shower*. It is used to stimulate depressed patients.

SHOCK THERAPY. In shock therapy the patient may experience anxiety beforehand, but during the actual treatment he feels neither pain nor discomfort. No one knows exactly how the benefits of shock therapy are produced. The fact remains that it has hastened the recovery of thousands of disordered minds which twenty-five years ago would have been pronounced incurable.

(1) *Insulin shock*. The drug is given by injection. It is used chiefly with schizophrenics. The dosage is gradually increased until the patient lapses into a coma. An injection of glucose or sugar administered by stomach tube restores him to consciousness.

(2) *Electro-shock*. It is now more common than insulin and easy to administer. Some hospitals maintain a shock therapy clinic where patients may obtain this treatment on an out-patient basis.

LOBOTOMY. In performing a lobotomy, the doctor attempts to sever some of the fibers connecting the front lobes of the brain with the emotional center of the brain. Doctors seldom advise this operation unless the chances of recovery by psychotherapy and shock treatment have been exhausted. If the patient is incurably ill, it may relieve him of his mental suffering or change his personality. Only lobotomy patients spend any time in bed. During the course of the other treatments, patients lead as active and normal a life as goes on in any institution.

Is prefrontal lobotomy morally permissible in the treatment of mental disorders? The principle to be applied in answering the question is this: any procedure harmful to the patient is morally justifiable only in so far as it is designed to produce a proportionate good. Seen in their totality, the results from lobotomy seem to point to more harm than good. Catholic hospitals may take the following as a guiding norm for competent physicians: Lobotomy is morally justifiable as a last resort in attempting to cure those who suffer from serious mental illness. It is not allowed when less extreme measures are reasonably available or in cases in which the probability of harm outweighs the probability of benefit. In weighing the factors pertinent to a moral judgment of the operation, it is well for us to realize that in skilled hands and with proper re-education, the lobotomized patient has a good chance of avoiding many of the possible evil effects of the operation. (See: Medico-Moral Problems, by Gerald Kelly, S.J., The Catholic Hospital Association of the United States and Canada.)

FAMILY CARE. This is the placement of convalescent mental cases in families other than their own. The patient and the family are matched as closely as possible in background, education, and religious beliefs. The homes are preferably rural. Ideally they are situated near a church and within walking distance of the kind of recreational facilities that the patient enjoys. The social worker visits regularly to see that standards are kept high. This is what is meant by the Gheel Plan used in Gheel, Belgium, the shrine of St. Dymphna.

WHAT YOU CAN DO

You can join with others in the fight against nervous and mental disorders by supporting those orgainzations that are working for the improvement of mental institutions. National organizations are developing nationwide programs of public education for the improvement of services to the mentally ill, such as the *National Committee for Mental Hygiene and the National Mental Health Foundation* (1520 Race Street, Philadelphia 2, Pa.). You can help by acquainting yourself with the truth about mental illness: how it develops, how it is treated, and how it can be prevented. You can see to it that your community provides facilities for prevention and early treatment. Good hospitals and clinics will come only when enlightened citizens see the need for them and are willing to spend the money it takes to operate them. In a democratic society each of us is responsible for all matters of public concern.

The work of alleviating the ills with which mankind is afflicted must be erected on the solid foundation of love of neighbor for the love of Christ. You can treat mentally ill persons as sick persons in need of sympathetic understanding and scientific, human care. You can convince others to take the same intelligent and Christian attitude.

Eminent psychiatrists and psychologists have indicated that a large number of patients could leave mental institutions if they could be assured of receiving a sympathetic reception in the world. Institutions can help certain cases only to a limited extent; after that they must necessarily depend on their fellow human beings in the outside world to help them find their place in normal life. You may not be able to duplicate the work of the people of Gheel, but you can certainly imitate their spirit and do whatever is possible as the occasions present themselves. You can look upon your suffering brethren with a Christian spirit of love and compassion and see in them the suffering Christ. You can learn from contemplating them, that the things of this world are passing, and that you must not make this earthly existence the center of your happiness. Perhaps then you will better be able to bear your own crosses and sufferings and more willingly help your neighbor who may be groaning under his.

You can assist the mentally ill *by visiting* the most friendless patients. Some unfortunates never have a visitor; their families have completely abandoned them. Often they are aged fathers and mothers who are not insane, but childish. A friendly smile, a sympathetic word, a little, inexpensive gift will do wonders to help brighten the drab lives of these people. Doctors maintain that such kindnesses are oftentimes more beneficial than any medical treatment which they can prescribe. Various parish societies might find it possible to give parties in the wards occasionally.

Above all, you can *pray* for those mentally ill and encourage others, especially the friends and relatives of those thus afflicted, to do the same. *Acquaint them with the devotion to Saint Dymphna by distributing copies of this pamphlet.* Greater things are wrought by prayer than this world dreams of! Where medical science fails, prayer will succeed, for we are all in the care of our omnipotent Creator and loving Father.

You *are* your brother's keeper. Some eight million persons who are mentally ill can profit from your charitable concern. Some of them are your neighbors, your friends, and your relatives. Our Lord's words ring true especially for them: "As long as you did it for one of these, the least of my brethren, you did it for me" (Matt. 25, 40).

Order More Of The Same

THE CANCER SAINT — St. Peregrine, 5c
THE TB SAINT — St. Thérèse, 5c
THE HEART SAINT — St. John of God, 10c

Divine Word Missionary Publications
THE MISSION PRESS, TECHNY, ILL.

IMPRIMI POTEST

Robert C. Hunter, S.V.D., Provincial, Girard, Pa.

NIHIL OBSTAT

A. H. Wiersbinski, LL.D., Censor Librorum

IMPRIMATUR

✛ John Mark Gannon, D.D., D.C.L., LL.D., Bishop of Erie

CPSIA information can be obtained
at www.ICGtesting.com
Printed in the USA
LVHW021616091122
732754LV00004B/224

9 781013 489365